Help your friend if he asks for it.

Be able to say, "I'm sorry."

Be helpful.

Have them over to your house.

Tell them they are good at something.

Share.

Let them play in your game.

Help them clean up their room.

Share things—like your lunch.

Compliment them.

Take them places.

Be generous.

Say, "Good job."

Be considerate.

If you have something you don't want, give it to your friend.

Take turns.

Ways to Be a Friend

Smile.

Talk to your friend.

These ideas were contributed by Mr. B.'s third grade class, Derby Academy, fall 1996.

If your friend gets hurt, bring her to a teacher.

Call them by the names they want to be called.

Read a word if they can't.

Don't argue.

Play together.

Cooperate.

Respect something your friend does.

When they're upset, comfort them.

If they lose in a game, say, "Good game!" instead of bragging.

Invite them to play with you.

Try to agree.

Respect their privacy.

If they are discouraged, cheer them up.

Laurie Krasny Brown and Marc Brown

HOW TO BE A
FRIEND

A Guide to Making Friends
and Keeping Them

LITTLE, BROWN AND COMPANY
New York · Boston

For
Maria Modugno

Acknowledgments
Special thanks for their comments and criticism to our
expert readers: Edwin Bartholomew, third grade teacher; Linda Braun,
executive director of Families First Parenting Programs; Dorothy Burlage,
Ph.D., clinical psychologist; Bernice Hawkins, second grade teacher; Phyllis
Oppenheim, special education teacher; Polly Rizzotto, kindergarten teacher;
Judie Stolp, head of lower school; Phyllis Wender, literary agent; and
Denise Yocum, Psy.D., school counselor, Powell Associates.

Little, Brown and Company

Hachette Book Group USA
237 Park Avenue, New York, NY 10017
Visit our Web site at www.lb-kids.com

First Paperback Edition

Brown, Laurene Krasny
   How to be a friend : a guide to making friends and keeping them
/ Laurie Krasny Brown and Marc Brown. – 1st ed.
      p.   cm.
   Summary: Dinosaur children illustrate the value of friends, how
to make friends, and how to be and not to be a friend.
   ISBN 0-316-10913-4 (hc) / ISBN 978-0-316-11153-9 (pb)
   1. Friendship in children — Juvenile literature. [I. Friendship.]
1. Brown, Marc Tolon.   II. Title.
BF723.F68B76   1998
158.2'5 — dc21   97-10179

            HC: 10   9   8
            PB: 10   9   8   7   6

                        SC

            Manufactured in China

Contents

Me, Myself, and I

There are times when it feels good to be by yourself, enjoying your own company.

You can think up ideas, pretend, and play exactly what you want.

With no one else around, you can have all the toys to yourself.

Who Can Be Your Friend?

But some games are too hard to play by yourself. And they're not as much fun all alone.

There are times when you may feel lonely or bored, when you want to have someone to play with.

Why don't you ask that boy to play?

At least try.

I'm scared to ask. What if he says no?

Anyone who is nice to you and who likes to play with you can become a friend.

Friends can be different from each other in all kinds of ways.

Hi! My name's Martha. What's yours?

My friend is good at the computer.

My baby-sitter is a friend.

My mom would be my friend, except she's already my mom.

He's my boyfriend.

9

But there is one important way
that friends are always alike.

Friends feel the same way about each other!

11

Ways to Be a Friend

There are many ways to show that you like someone and want to be a friend.

> Heads or tails?

You can play fair. Flip a coin with a friend to see who goes first.

> Stop it! Leave him alone!

You can protect a friend if someone starts bothering him.

> Four for you, four for me...

You can share toys and other things.

You can stand up for friends, even when other kids complain about them or make fun of them.

You can invite them to play with you.

You can listen to your friends and pay attention to what they say.

You can try to cheer up a friend who's feeling sad.

You can cooperate. Go along with *your friend's* ideas sometimes.

You can offer help to friends when they need it.

You can compliment your friend, even when she wins and you lose. That's being a good sport.

You can keep your word. Then friends will know that they can trust you.

You can do things for friends, like making them special presents.

Joining in the Fun

Everyone feels left out sometimes. And it's not always easy to join in.

> We don't need any more members.

> I will *too* play! Or else . . .

Feeling left out hurts inside. But acting too angry about it usually doesn't help.

Doing nothing isn't much help, either. You may end up feeling helpless and sad.

What you *can* do instead . . . is to invite someone else to play with you.

Want to play?

Or find something you like doing on your own for a while.

Later, you could try to join in the group again. If you watch to see what they are playing, you might be able to offer some help.

Do you guys need a clubhouse flag?

KEEP OUT

ME OF

Cool!

17

Feeling Shy

We all feel shy at times, such as when we meet new classmates or go to new places.

When you feel shy, it takes courage even to say hi to someone. But the more you practice, the easier it gets.

19

Ways *Not* to Be a Friend

Friends are bound to disagree about things. Even best friends can bother each other sometimes.

There are many ways to upset your friends.

If you cheat and don't follow the rules.

If you insult them or call them mean names.

If you don't let them play.

If you tease or make fun of them.

If you hit or hurt them.

20

If you don't share things.

If you don't let your friend play with anyone else.

If you act like a poor sport, showing off when you win or quitting so you won't lose.

If you blame friends for something they didn't do.

If you ignore what your friends say.

21

Bosses and Bullies

Being a boss means that you like to tell your friends what to do when you play. You like to make all the rules. But friends may get upset if you never let them have a chance to be in charge.

One of the worst ways to treat a friend is to act like a bully and try to scare someone into doing what you want.

If someone bullies you, *try* not to get upset. Tell the bully to leave you alone. Join other, friendly kids. If that doesn't work, ask a grown-up for help.

Making Up with a Friend

There is always more than one way to settle an argument. If you and your friend want to use the same toy, what could you do instead of fighting over it?

When I argue with a friend, Mom says, "Work it out." But how?

Be creative. Think of a way you both can use it.

One minute, five seconds, ten milliseconds left to ride . . .

Decide to take turns.

I'll run home and get my bike.

Okay. I'll go with you.

Try to get enough toys for both of you.

Make a deal. If *you* get what you want, what can your friend have?

If you *let* me ride your bike, I'll *let* you ride my skateboard.

Let's flip a coin to see who rides.

Heads or tails?

Use a trick such as flipping a coin or counting one-potato, two-potato to see who goes first.

I have two race cars. Want to play with them instead?

Okay. Next time I'll bring my bike.

Decide to play with something else.

Arguments

Arguments can make friends feel so angry, they can hardly think about making up . . . at least, not until they find a safe way to get out their anger.

27

Sometimes an argument just gets worse and worse, angrier and angrier, with no end in sight. Friends may need to separate, take time out, or get some grown-up help.

Oh, yeah!

Yeah!

Time out!
Looks like we need to make our talking circle.

Talking Out an Argument

Here are some steps to help you talk out an argument:

1 Stop arguing.

2 Calm down. Take deep breaths, count backwards, relax your muscles, or leave the group for a minute.

3 Agree to talk it out.

4 Everyone gets a turn to tell, not yell, their story and be listened to without interruptions.

5 Think up lots of ideas for solving the problem.

6 Try to choose the best solution, the one everyone agrees on and thinks will work.

7 Decide how to go about carrying out this plan.

8 Do it!

9 Remember, arguments are allowed, but meanness is not!

Remember:
In order to please everyone at least a little, you may not get exactly what you want.

Being Friendly

Being friendly means showing that you care about other kids, even the ones you hardly know. You can make them feel important and help them to belong.

It means treating others the way you would like them to treat you!

31

It feels great to have a friend!

say, "Ha, ha, you can't do that."

Bite them; push them.

Lie to them.

Boss them around.

say, "So what?" when they win an award.

Scream.

Ways Not to Be a Friend

Call them a name they don't like.

Make mean faces.

Be a poor sport.

Dump them.

Talk behind their backs.

Brag a lot.

Ignore them.

These ideas were contributed by
Mr. B.'s third grade class,
Derby Academy, fall 1996.

Don't help them when they have a problem.

Tell someone else whom he or she likes.

Say, "I don't like you."

Don't let them in your gym group.

Be mean to them.

If you can do something and your friend can't, make a big deal about it.

Tell them they can't play your game.

Hurt them or say they stink.

Tell someone else one of their secrets.

Say to your friend, "I have this and you don't!"

Make fun of them.